Dear Special, Amazing, Wonderful Person (PSST. That's you!),

Hello, and welcome to Night of the Sugar Skulls: A Coloring Story. This story hasn't been written in words because the illustrations are meant to guide you through the story and allow you to put your own interpretation(s) on them. Remember, what is most important between these pages is what you get out of the experience.

Whatever it is you need, whether it's a few minutes of downtime, to pay a visit to the blissful nostalgia of childhood crafts, or a path to meditation that doesn't put you to sleep. Or...

Maybe you need an outlet? Is your job stressful? Have you lost someone you loved or something important? Are you a slave to anxiety? We all need to find coping strategies for life's hiccups (big and small). Coloring is a great way to do that. Why? Because it's an escape...

As you color in these pages, you may lose yourself in the simple joy of letting loose your own inner artiste. Even if you're not all that creative, you may find peace and pleasure in this activity. Allow yourself to let go of fear, worry, regret, guilt, and grief as you bring life to these pages with your own imagination. Let a zen-like calm come over your entire being while you add texture and dimension to each flower, leaf and stem.

Included in this book are a few "clean canvas" skulls. I hope you have a blast decorating these skulls with your own embellishments and ornamentation. I hope you'll share these pages with me, or any of the pages here that you've colored in, by going to my Facebook page at: www.Facebook.com/natalieborges.art

TIPS:
I formatted this coloring book so that there is a blank page on the back-side of each illustration. Since I'm not making these books by hand, I cannot guarantee the thickness or quality of the paper. I recommend using colored pencils only; however, if you truly wish to use felt tip or other mediums, I would recommend placing a sheet of computer paper between the page you're coloring and the one behind (to prevent bleed through). Feel free to scan the images of your choice and re-print them on thicker paper for your own coloring/painting enjoyment. I personally find that a paper weight of 90lbs+ is sufficient for felt pens and minimal water-color painting.

Note:
This book has 26 illustrations that were hand-drawn and digitized by me. The art in this book is inspired by Dia De Los Muertos also known as "The Day of the Dead". These drawings are a work of fiction and do not represent real people (well, except for my renditions of Frida Kahlo), nor do they fully capture the beauty and power of Dia De Los Muertos. I have a deep love for the rich vibrance of Mexican art and culture and hope I have done them justice with my whimsical, dream-world.

Thank you, from the bottom of my heart, for purchasing this book and giving your creative spark a chance to shine.

Xoxo,
Natalie

Visit www.natalieborges.com
and www.Facebook.com/natalieborges.art

This coloring book is dedicated to my daughter. Thank you for your patience with Mommy while she was rediscovering and chasing her dreams. I hope to grow into the kind of woman you will admire and is deserving of your love. Chase your own dreams fiercely and without hesitation, with all the passion and emphatic joy that lives within your heart.

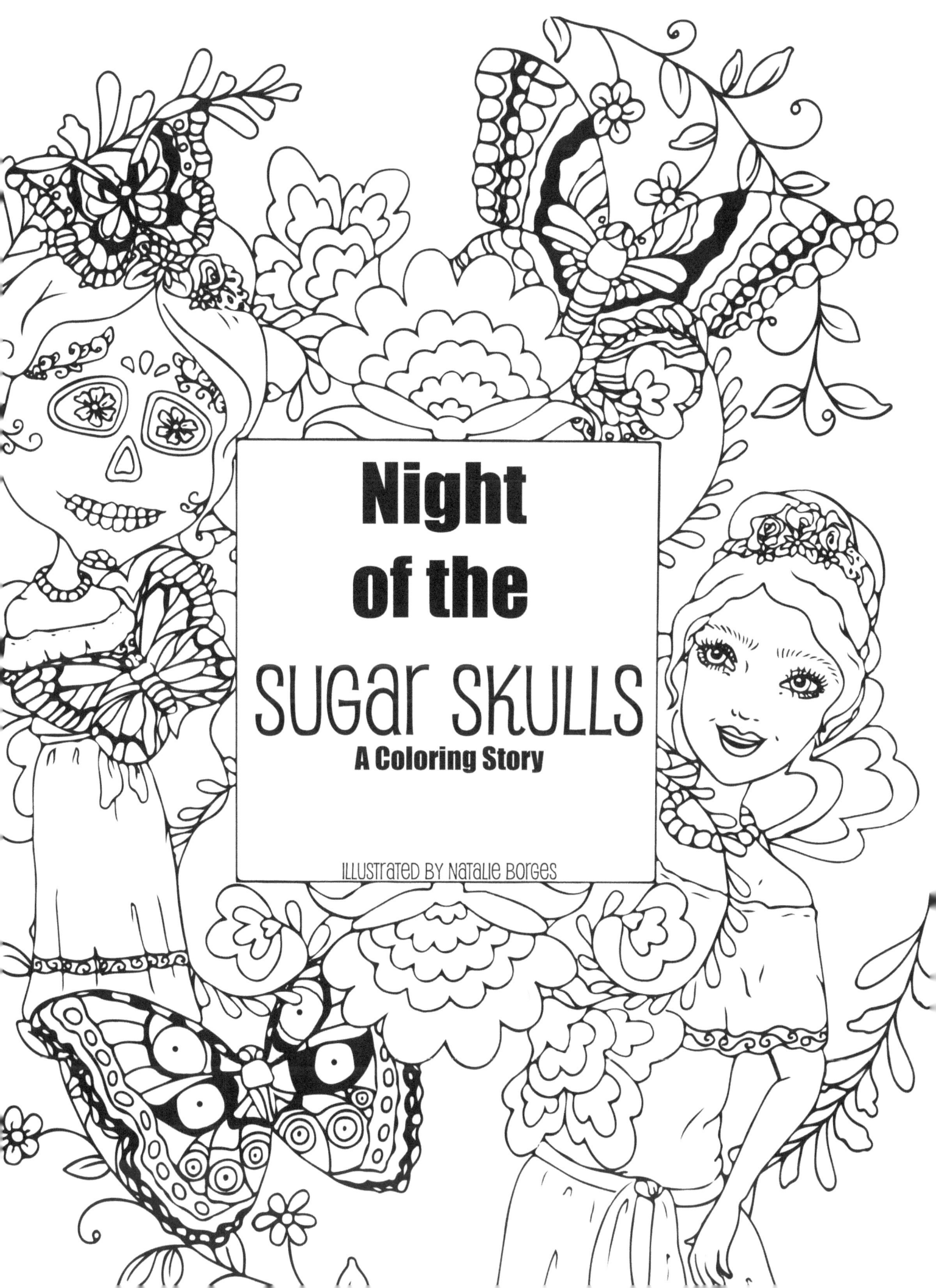

Night of the

SUGAR SKULLS

A Coloring Story

ILLUSTRATED BY Natalie Borges

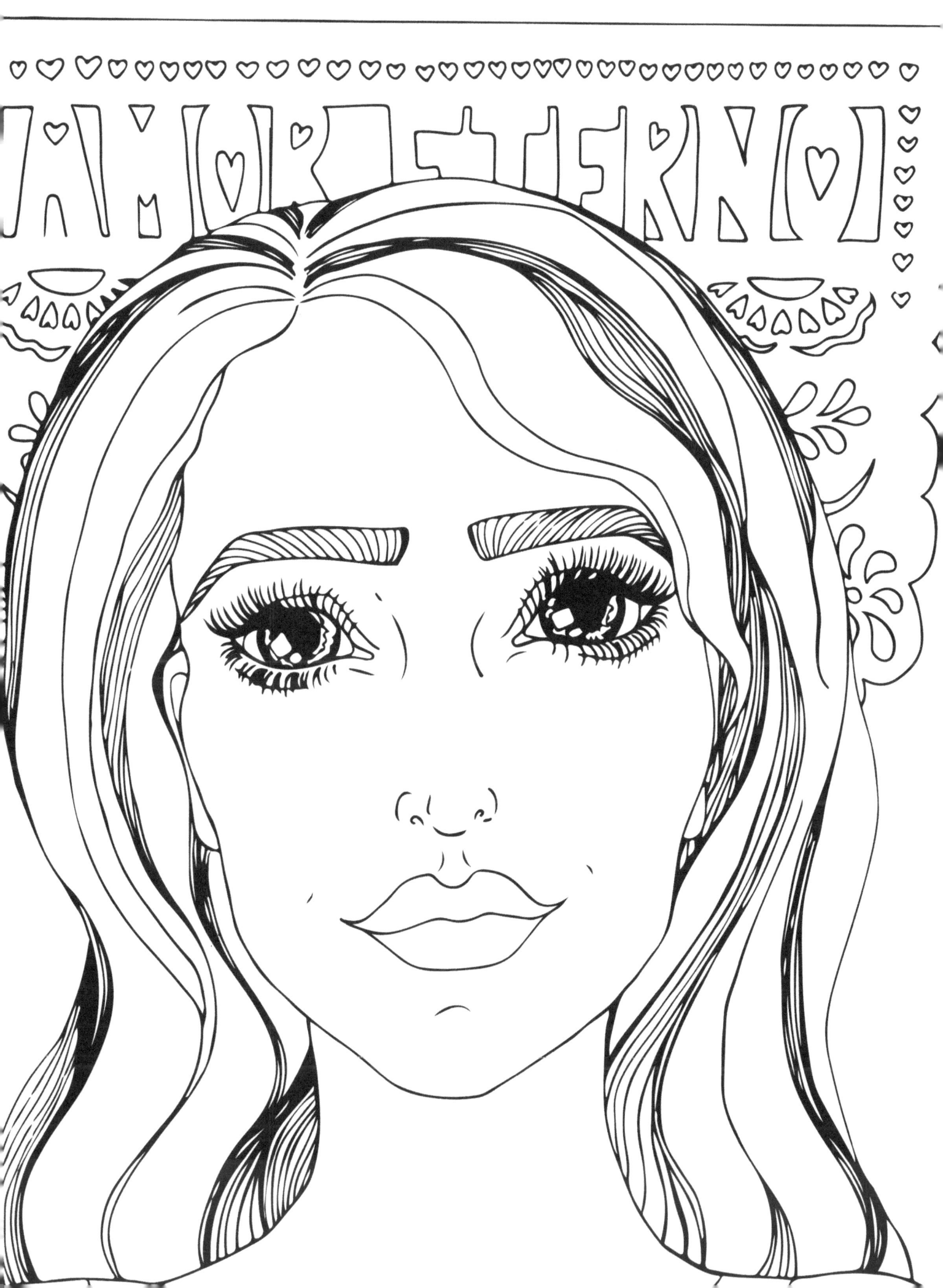

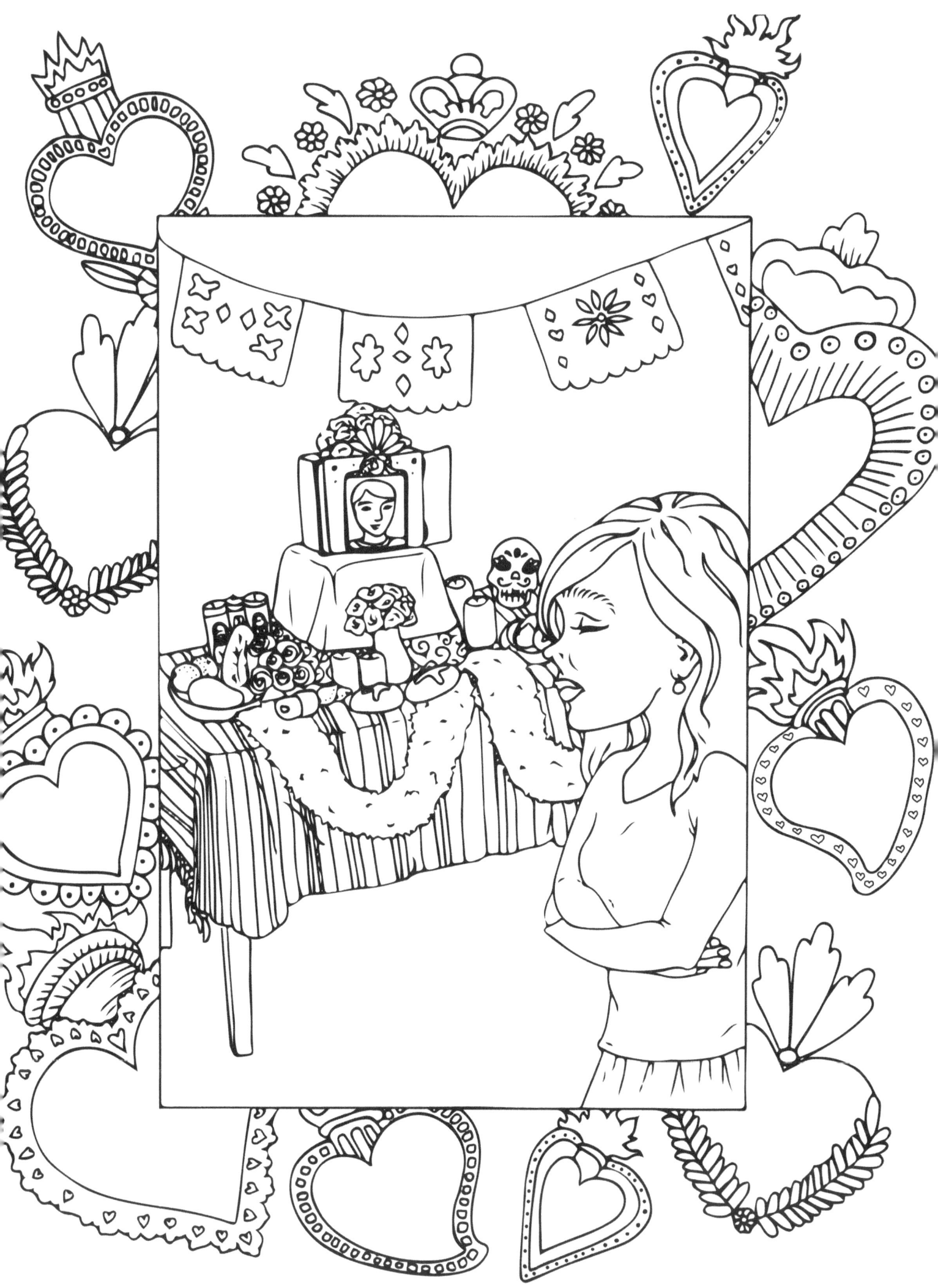

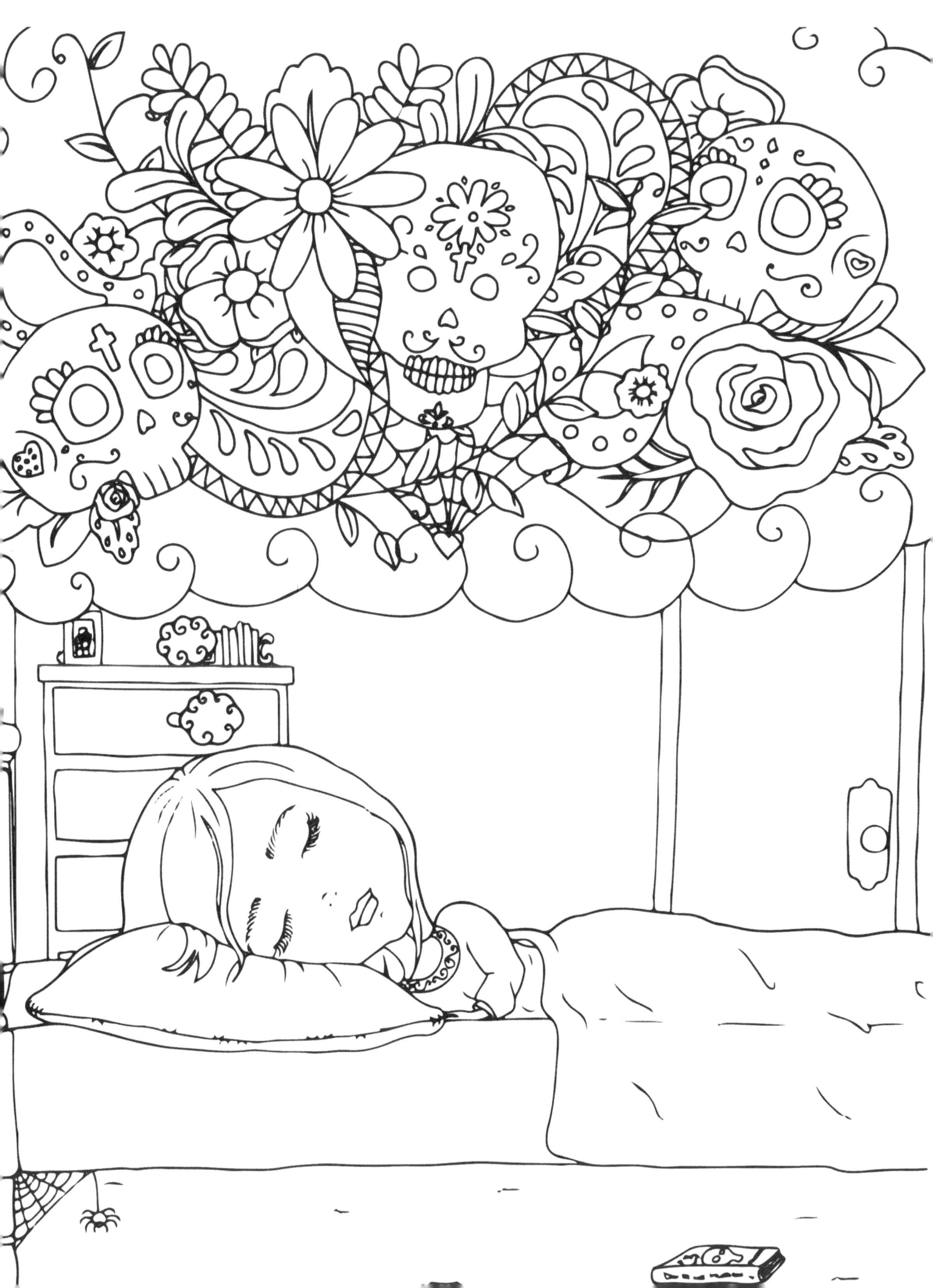

14

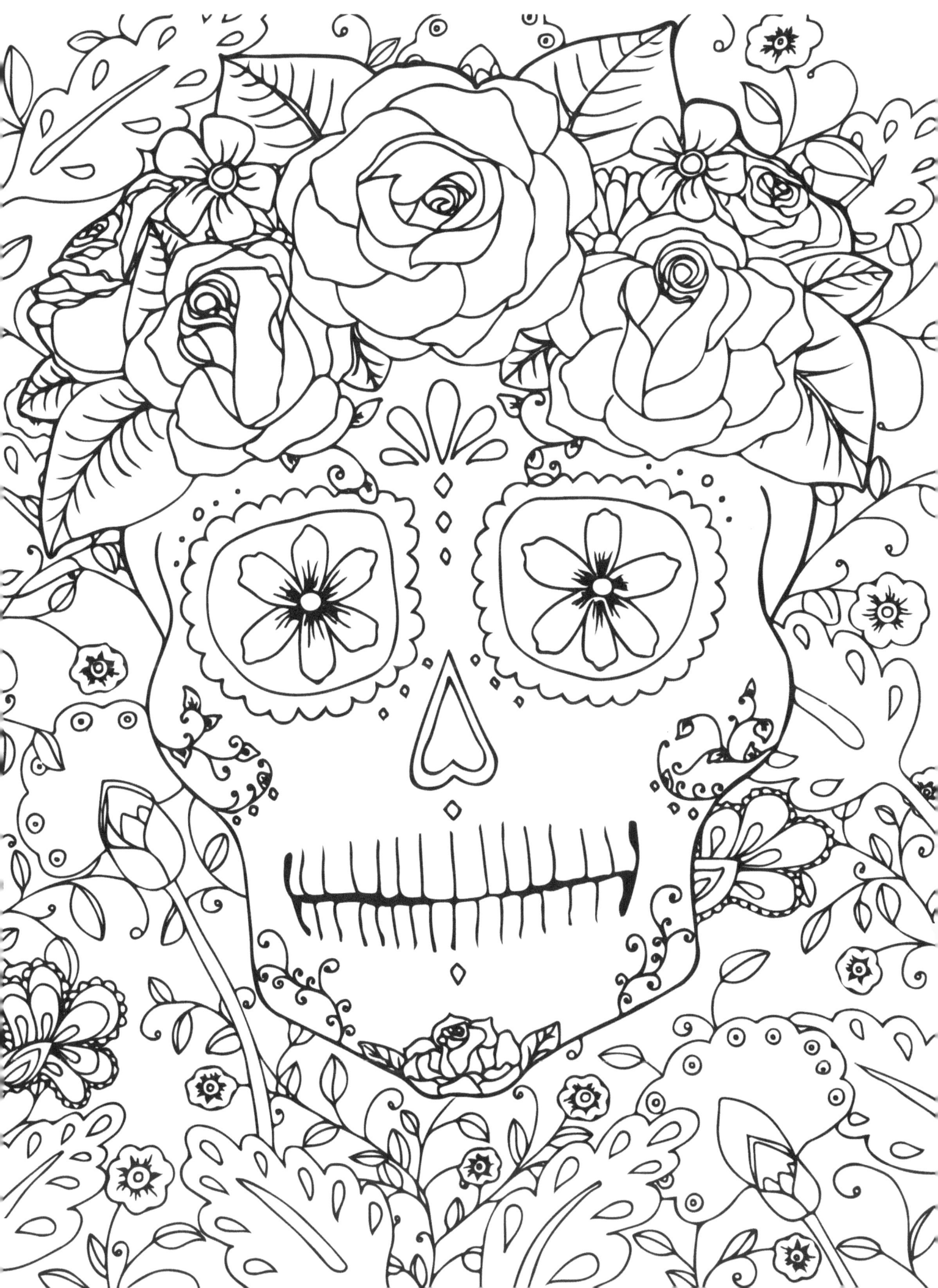

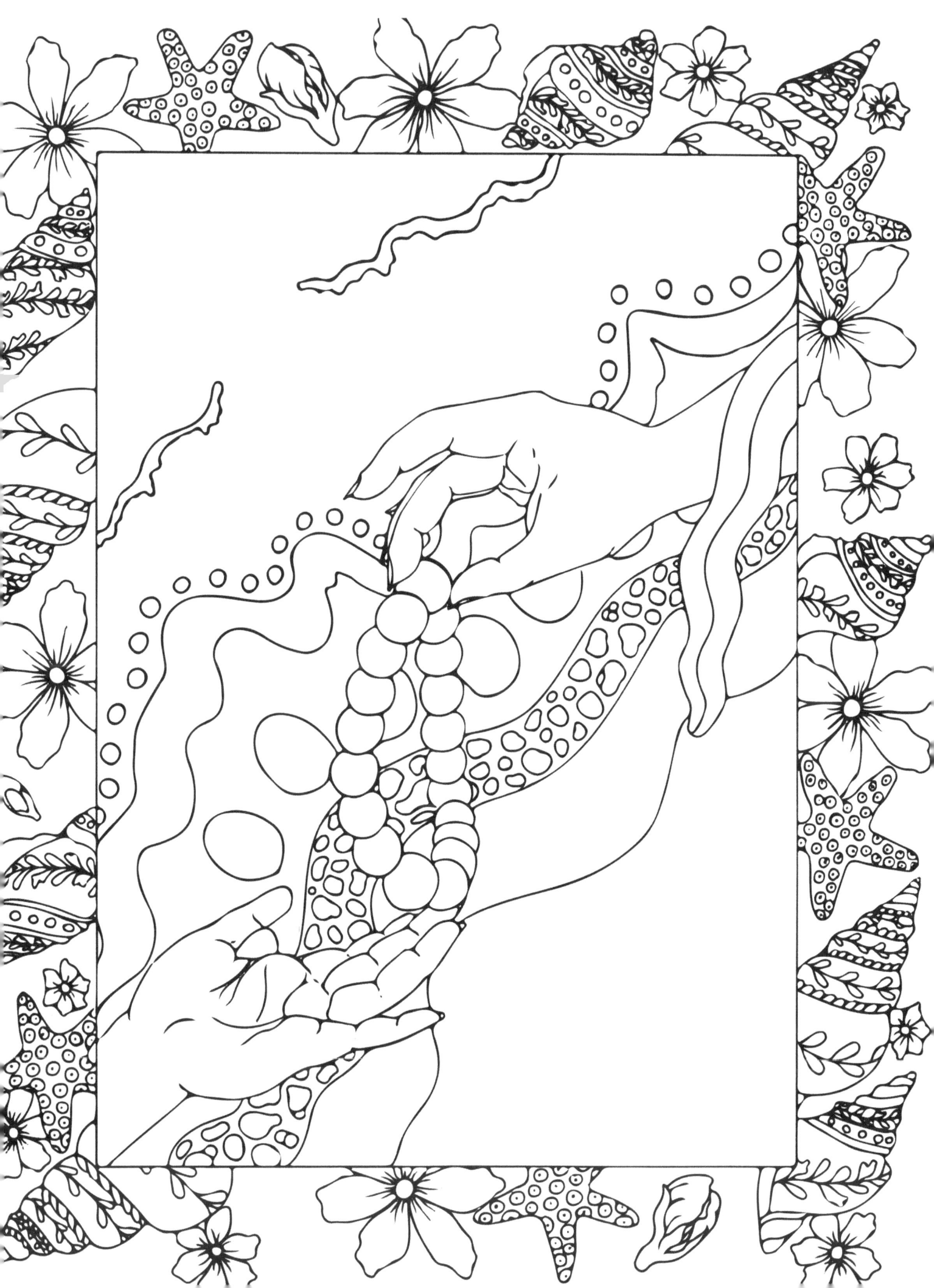

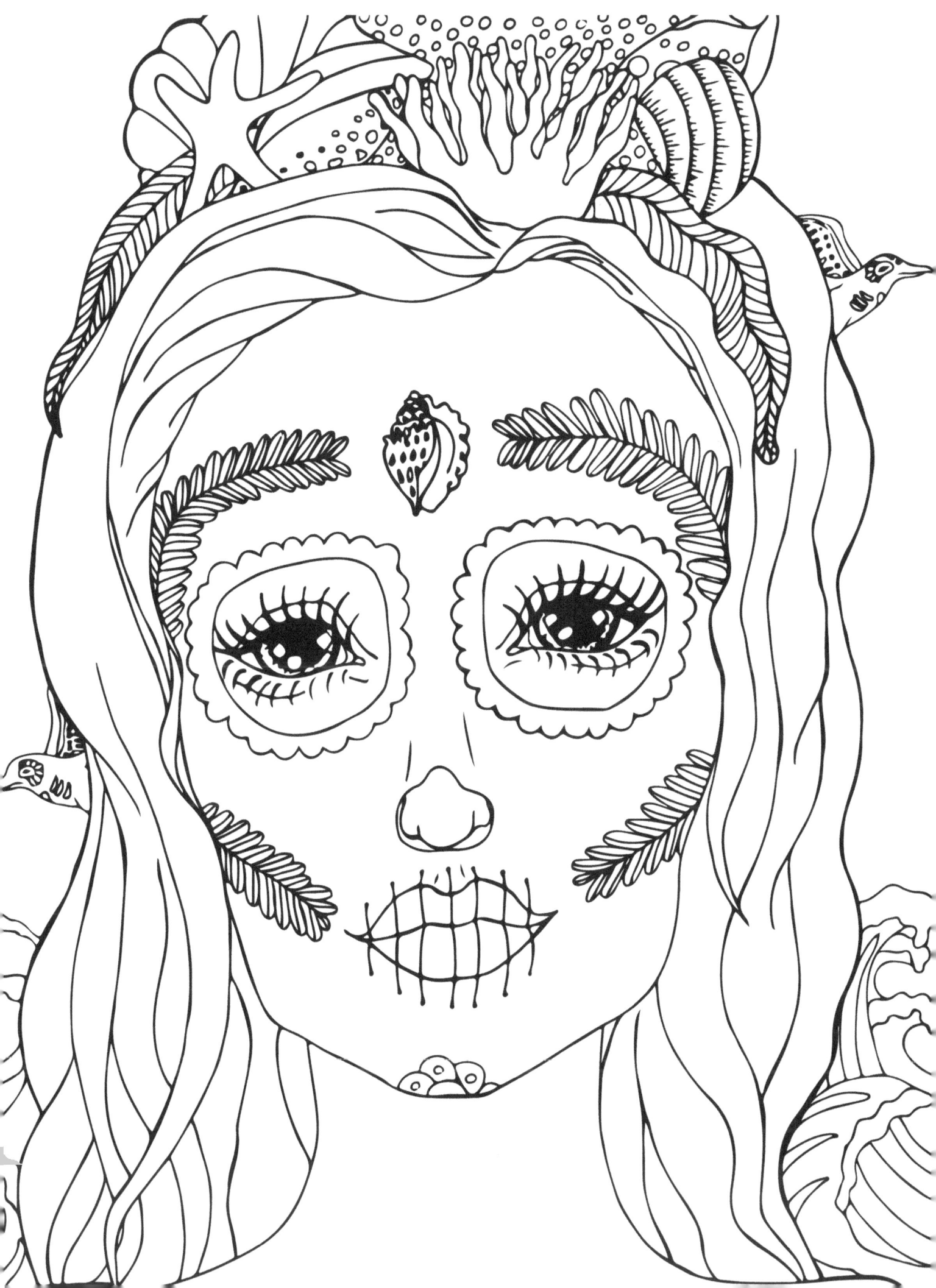

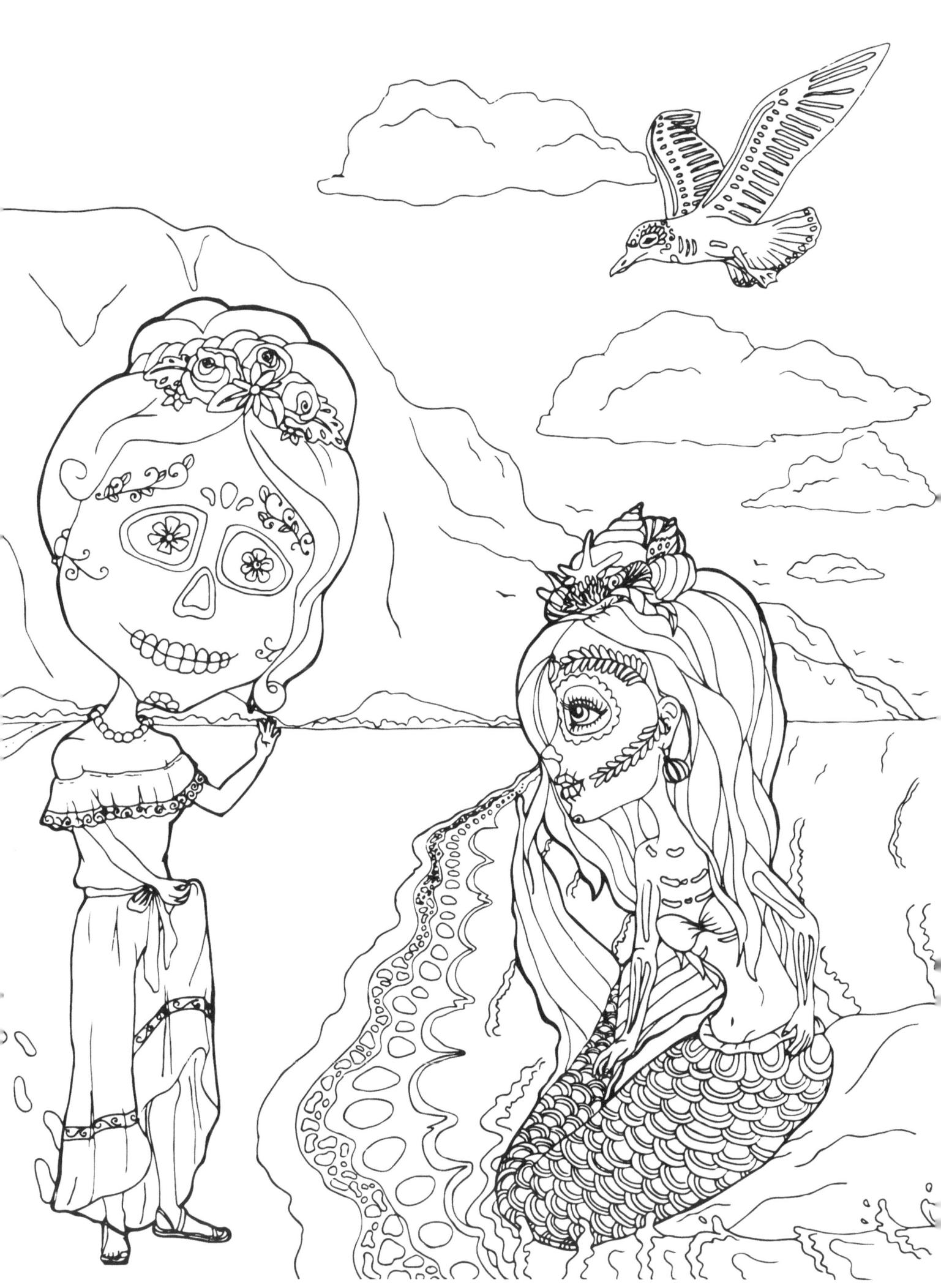

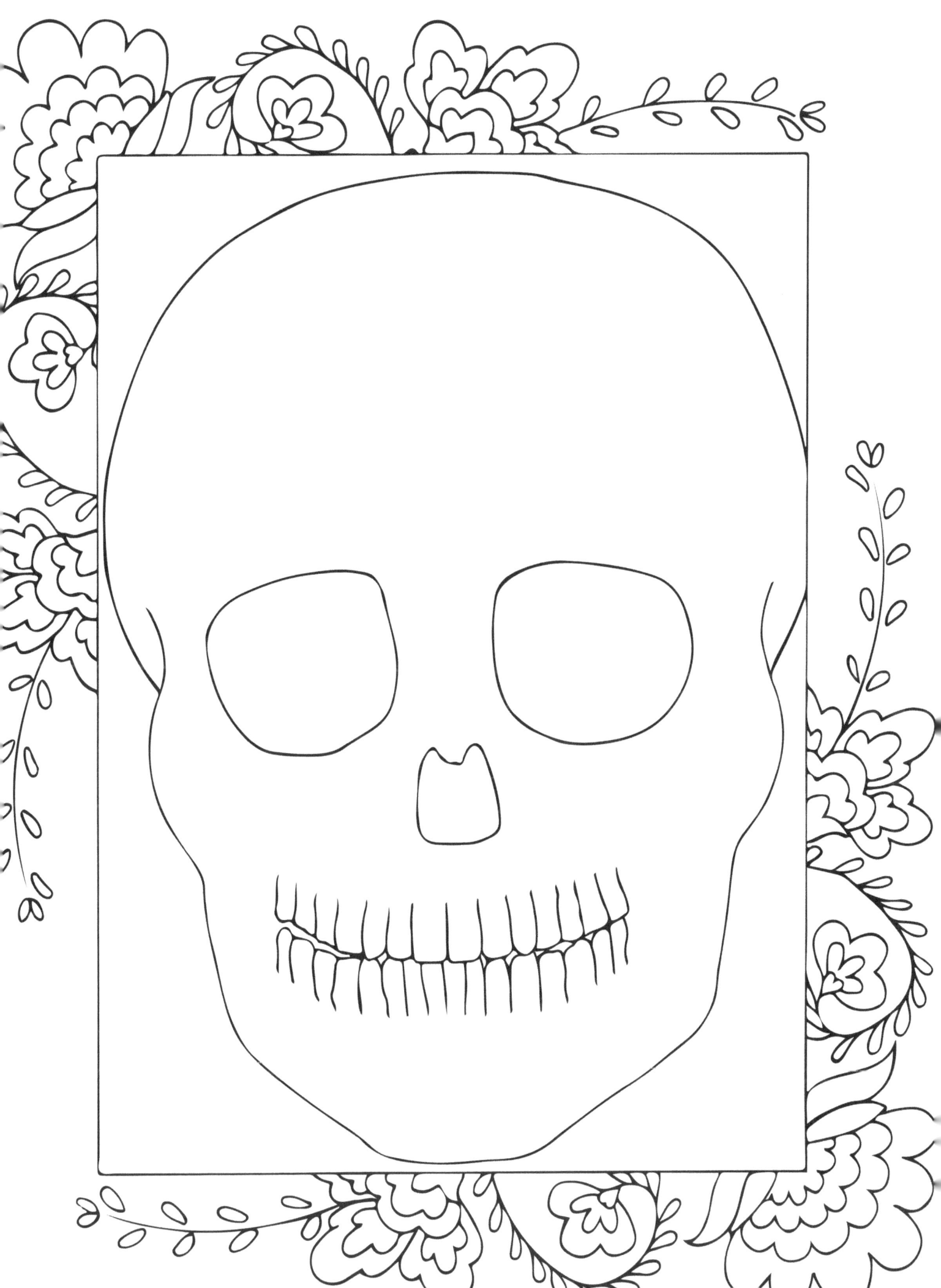

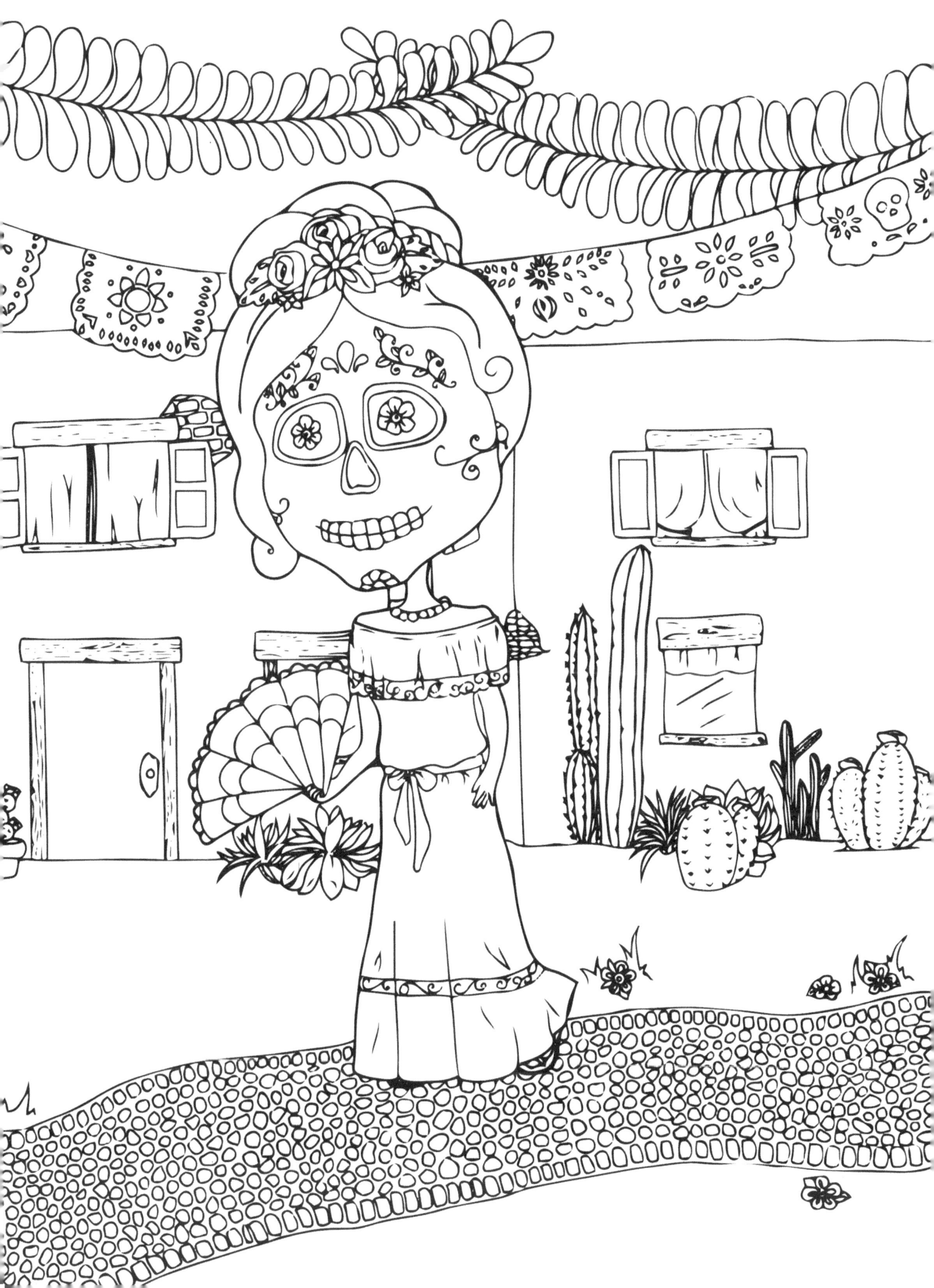

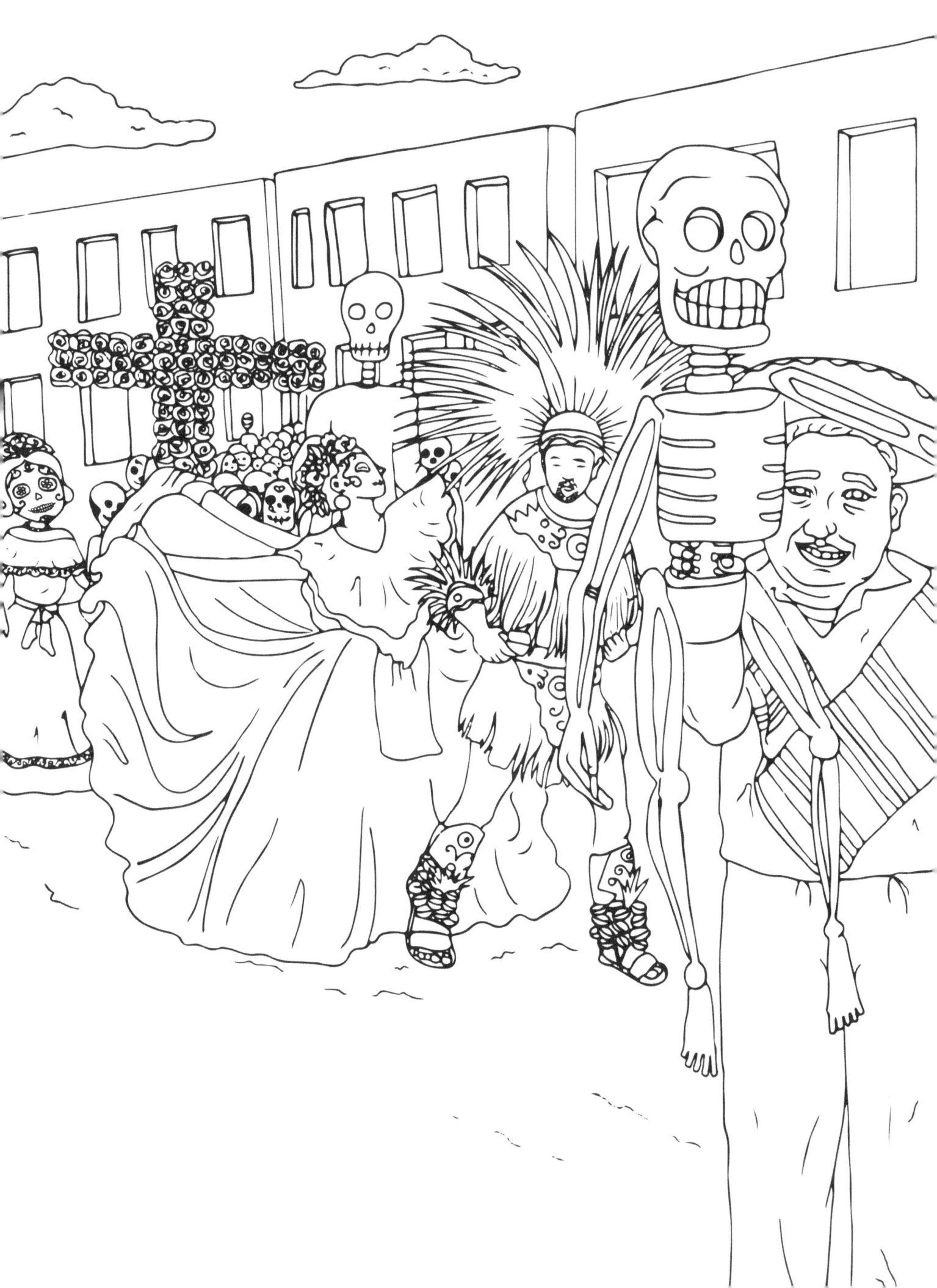

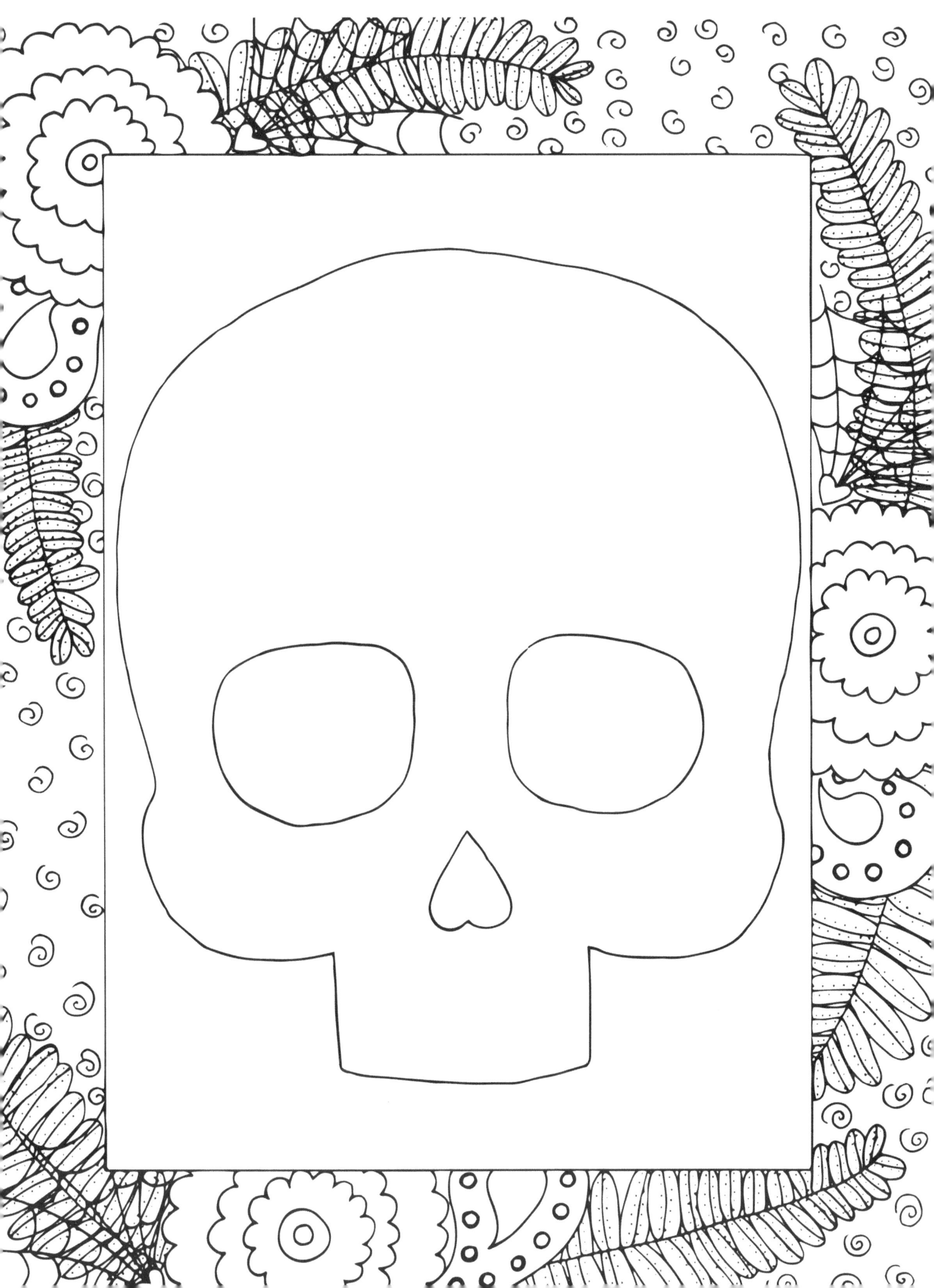

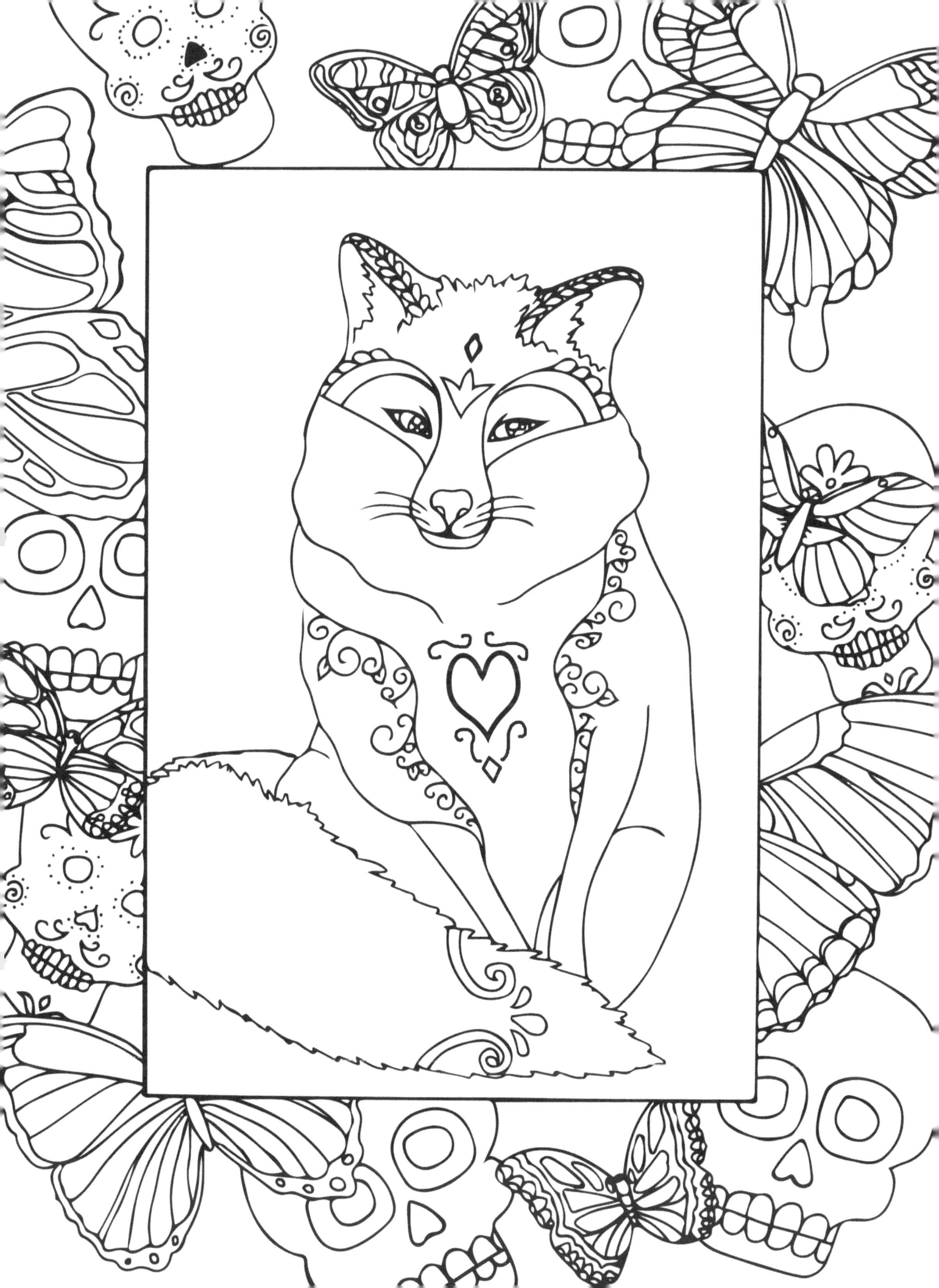

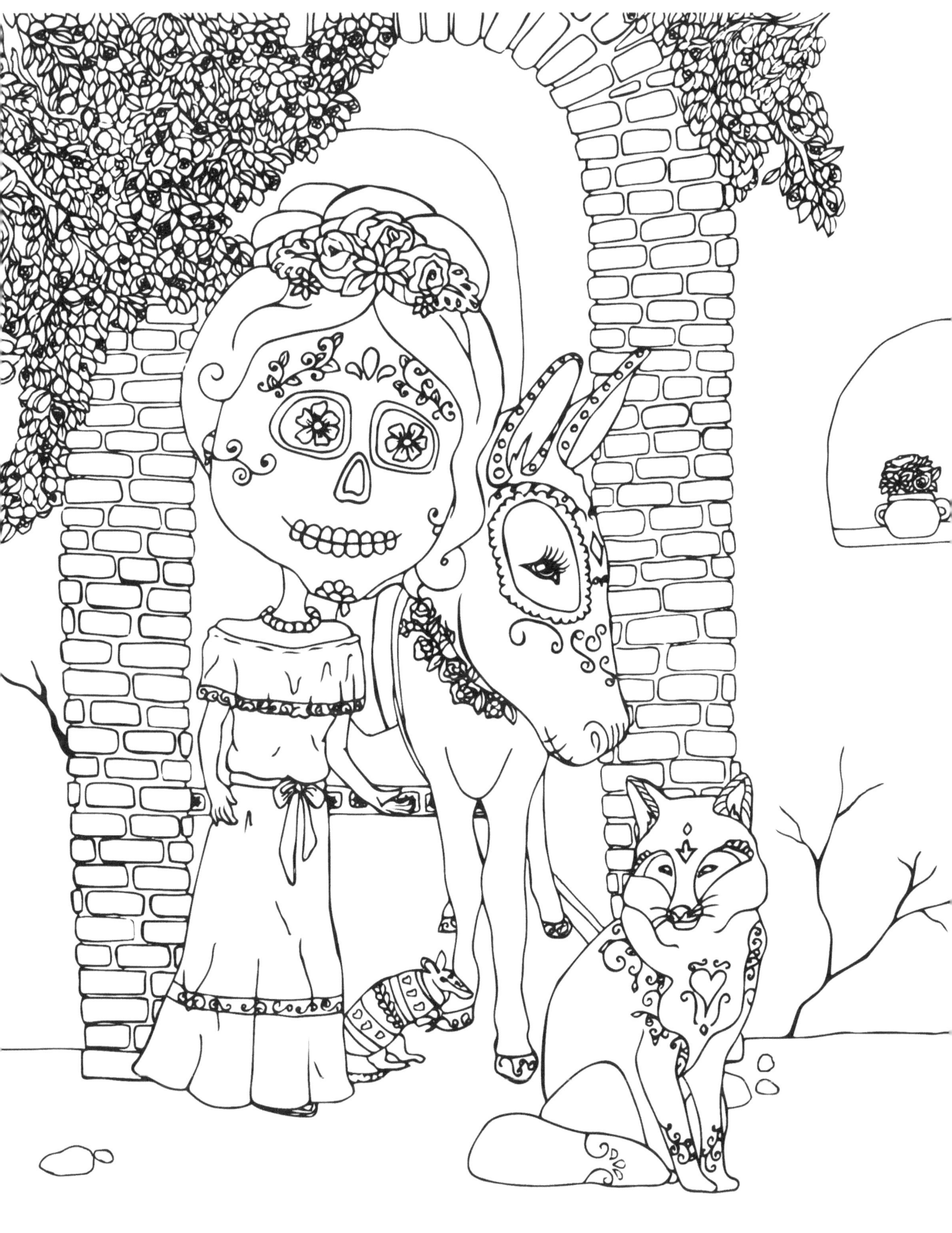

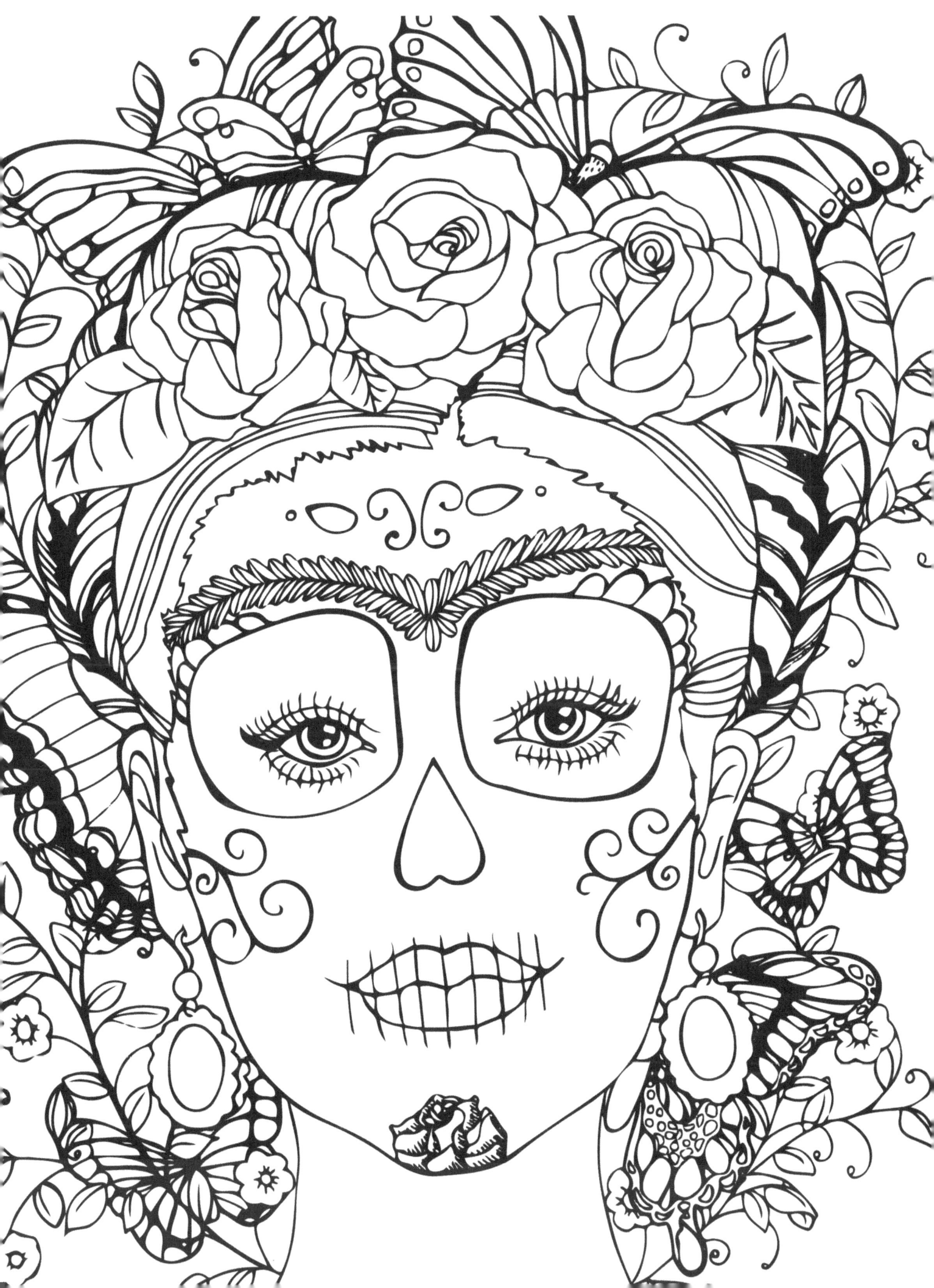

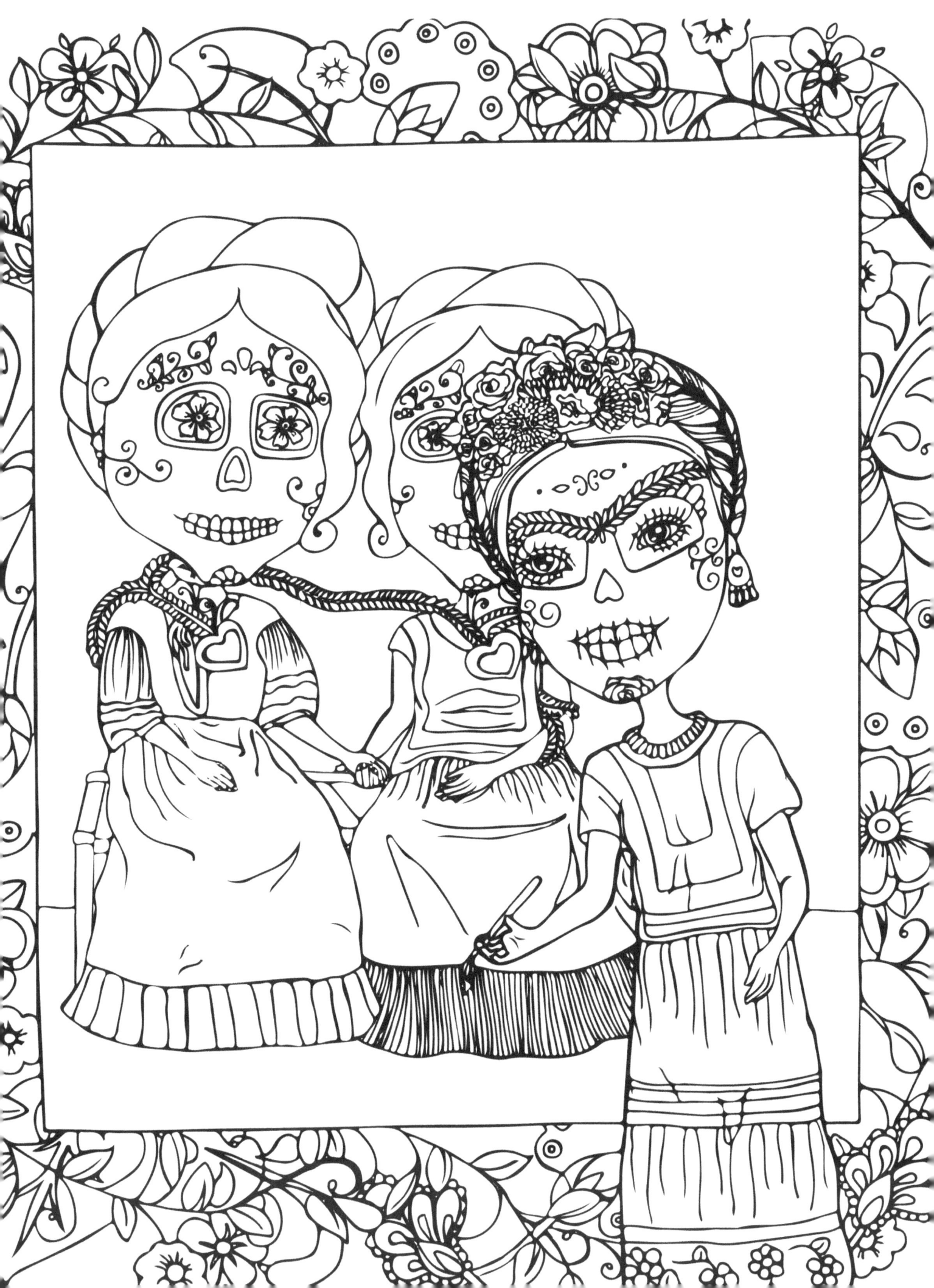

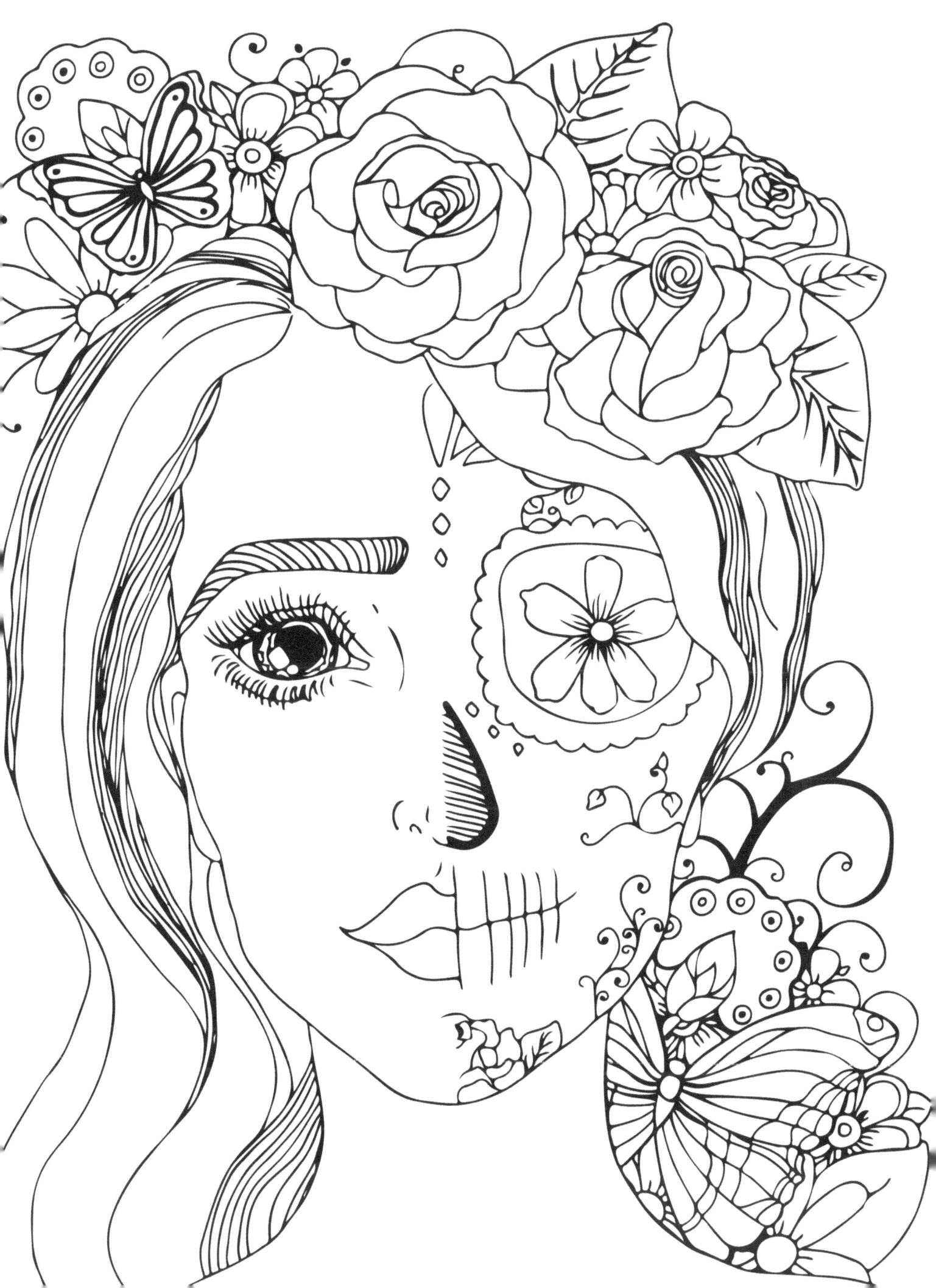

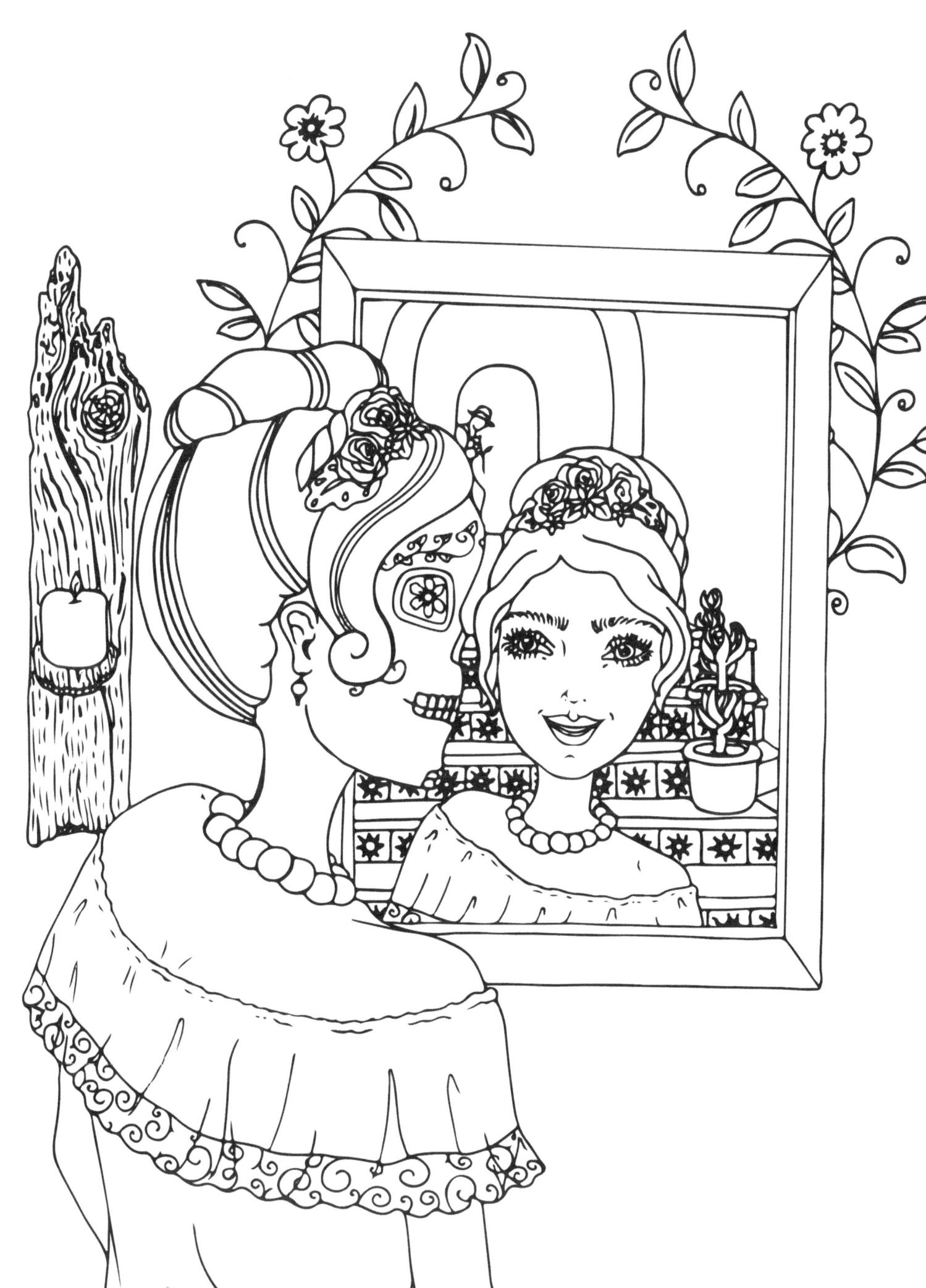

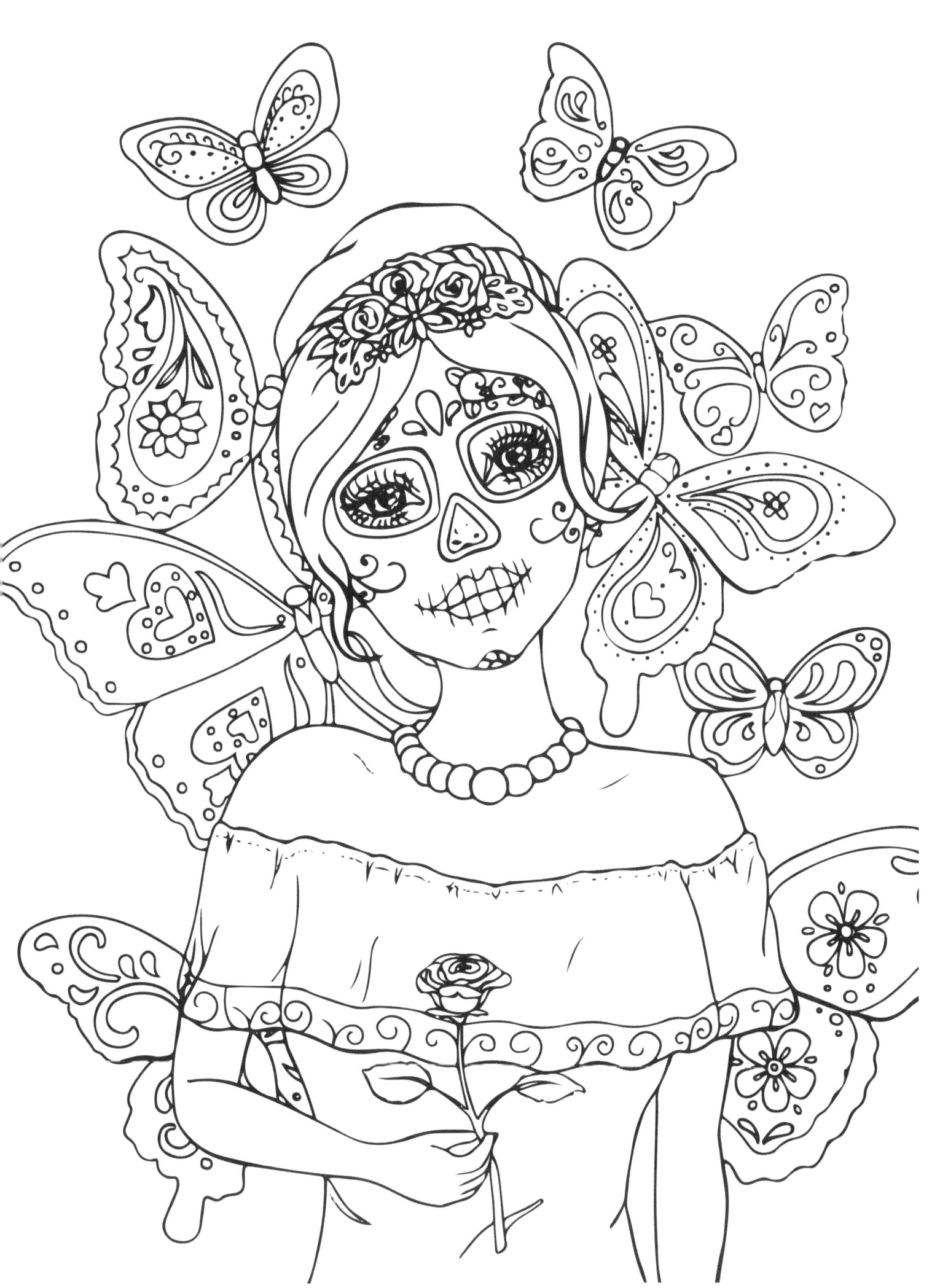

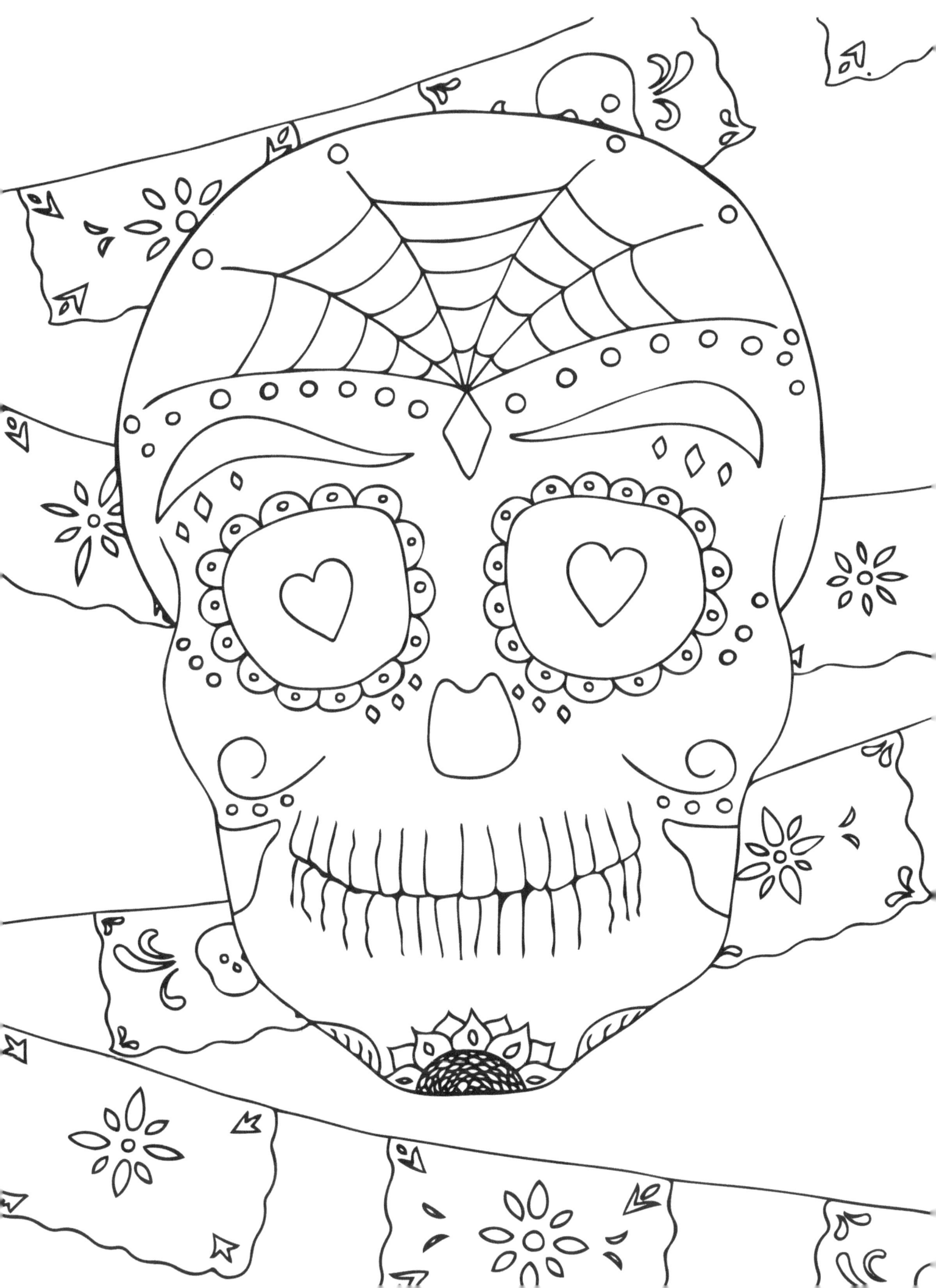

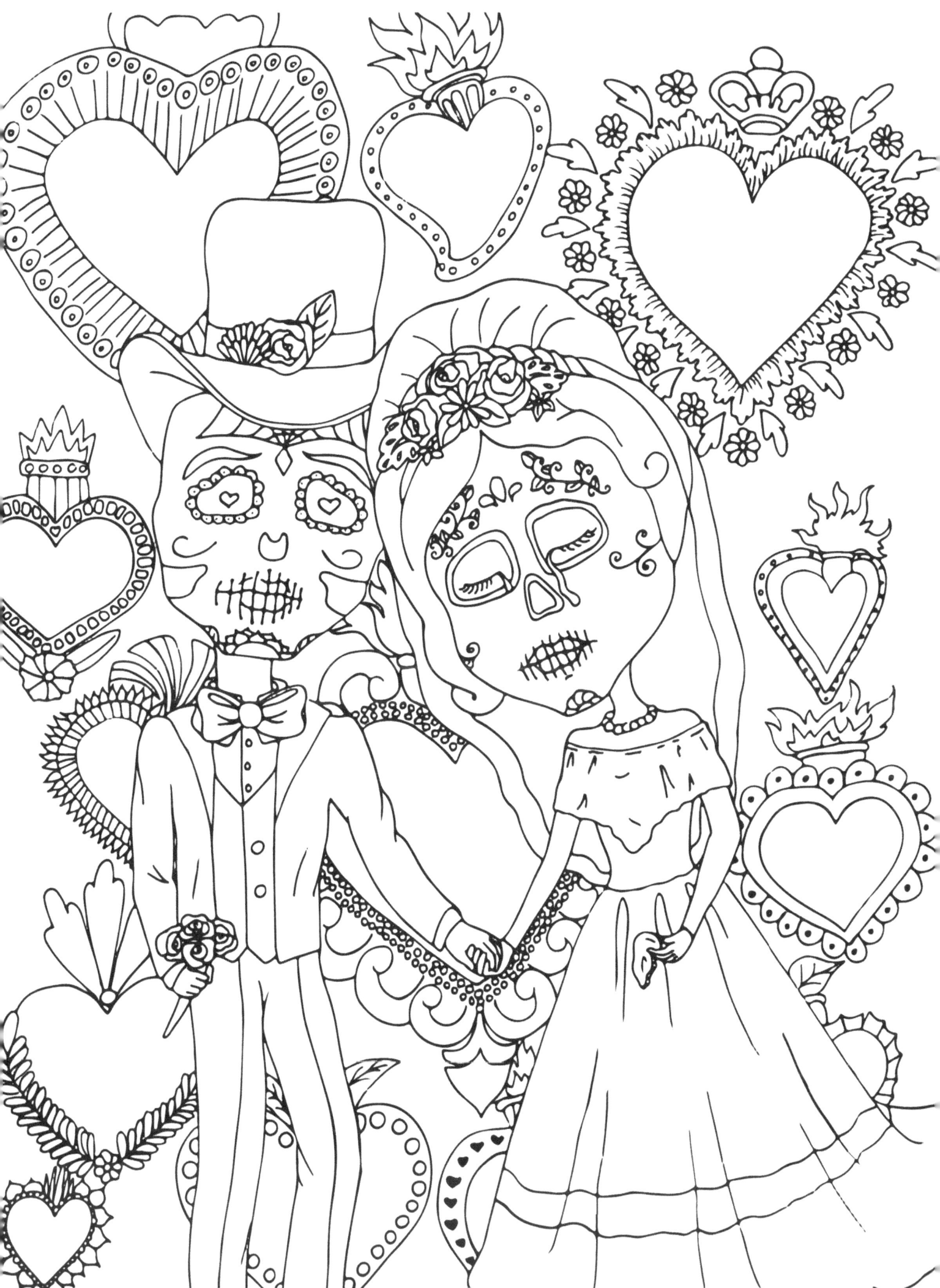

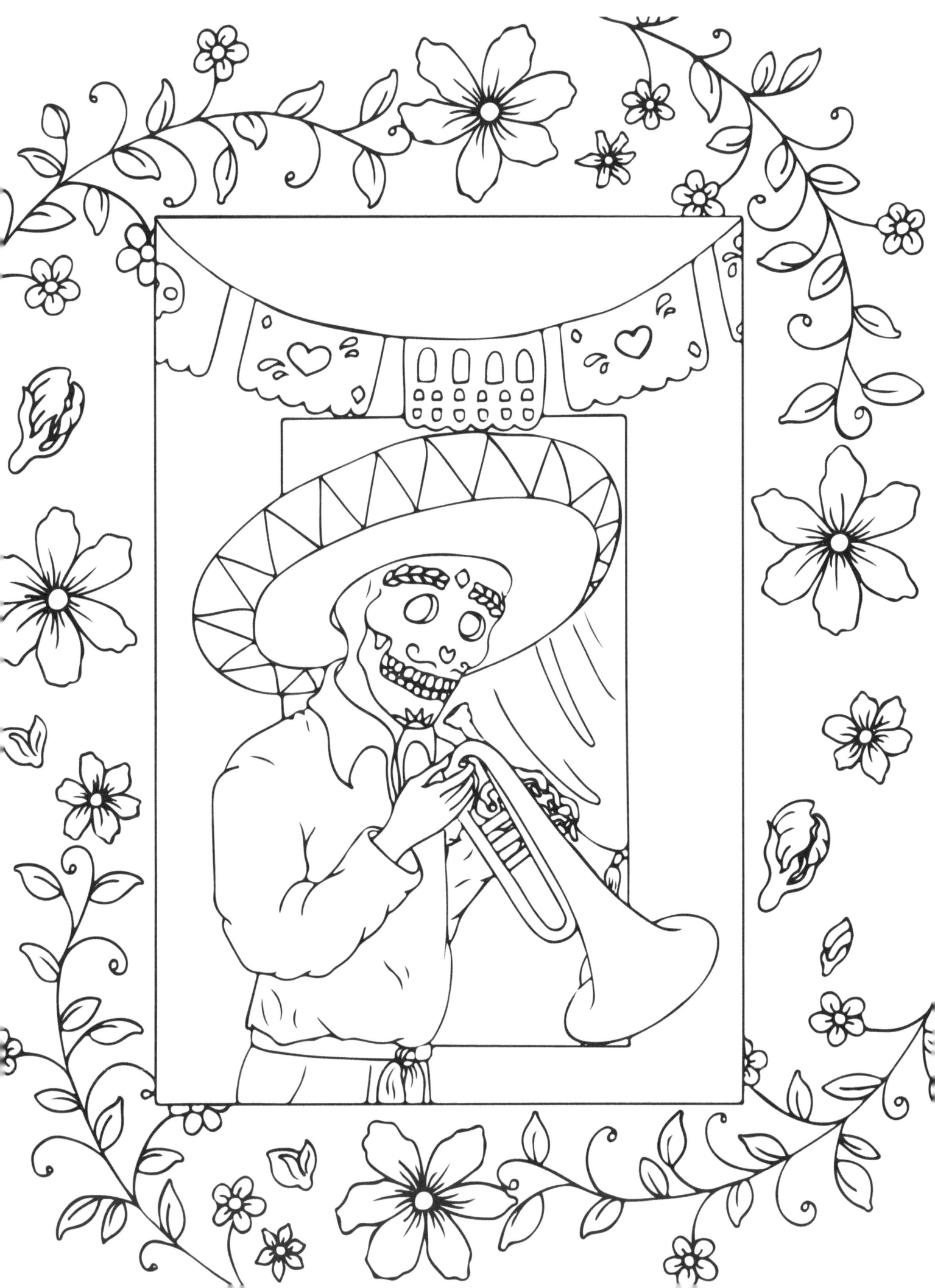

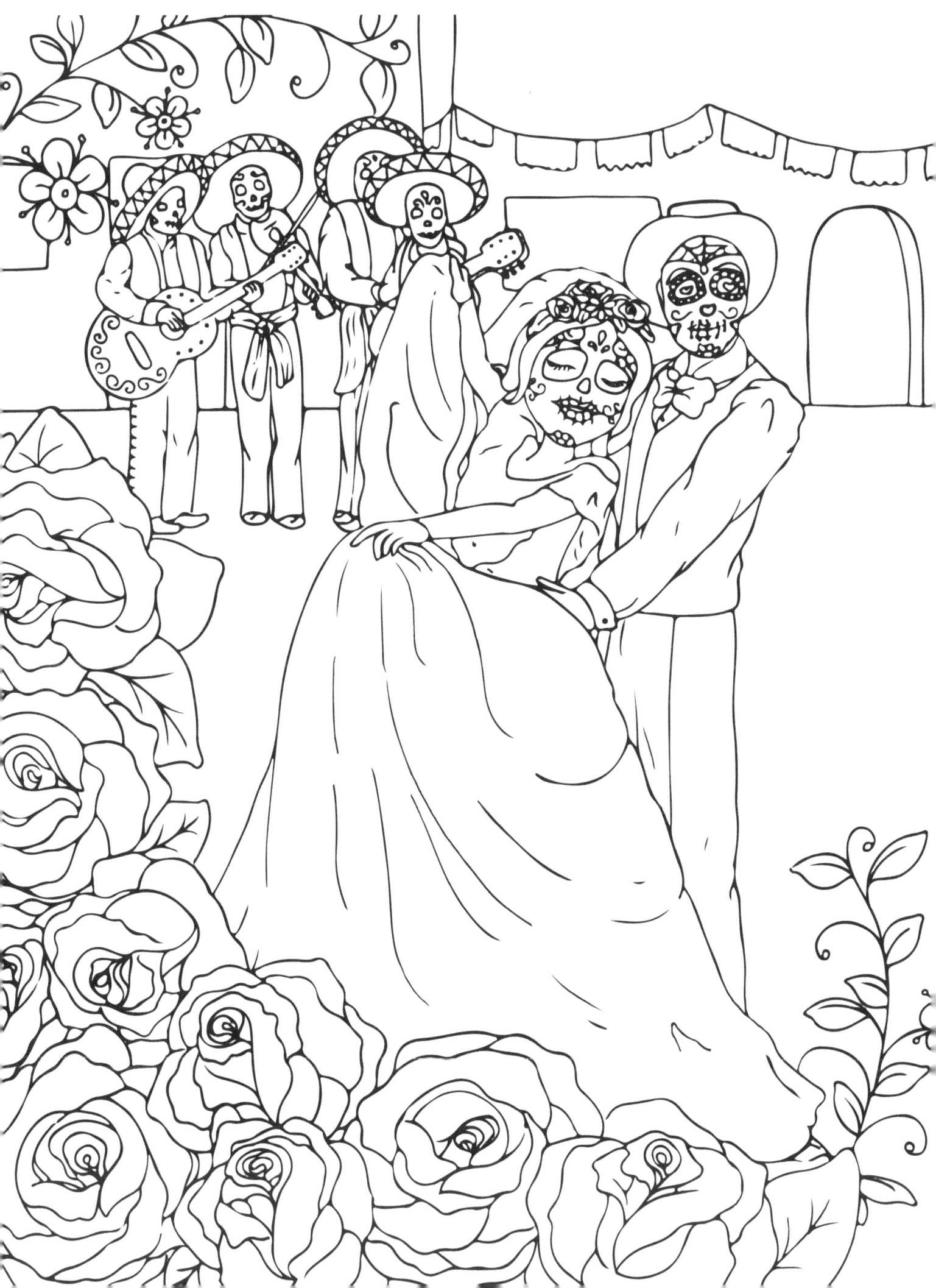

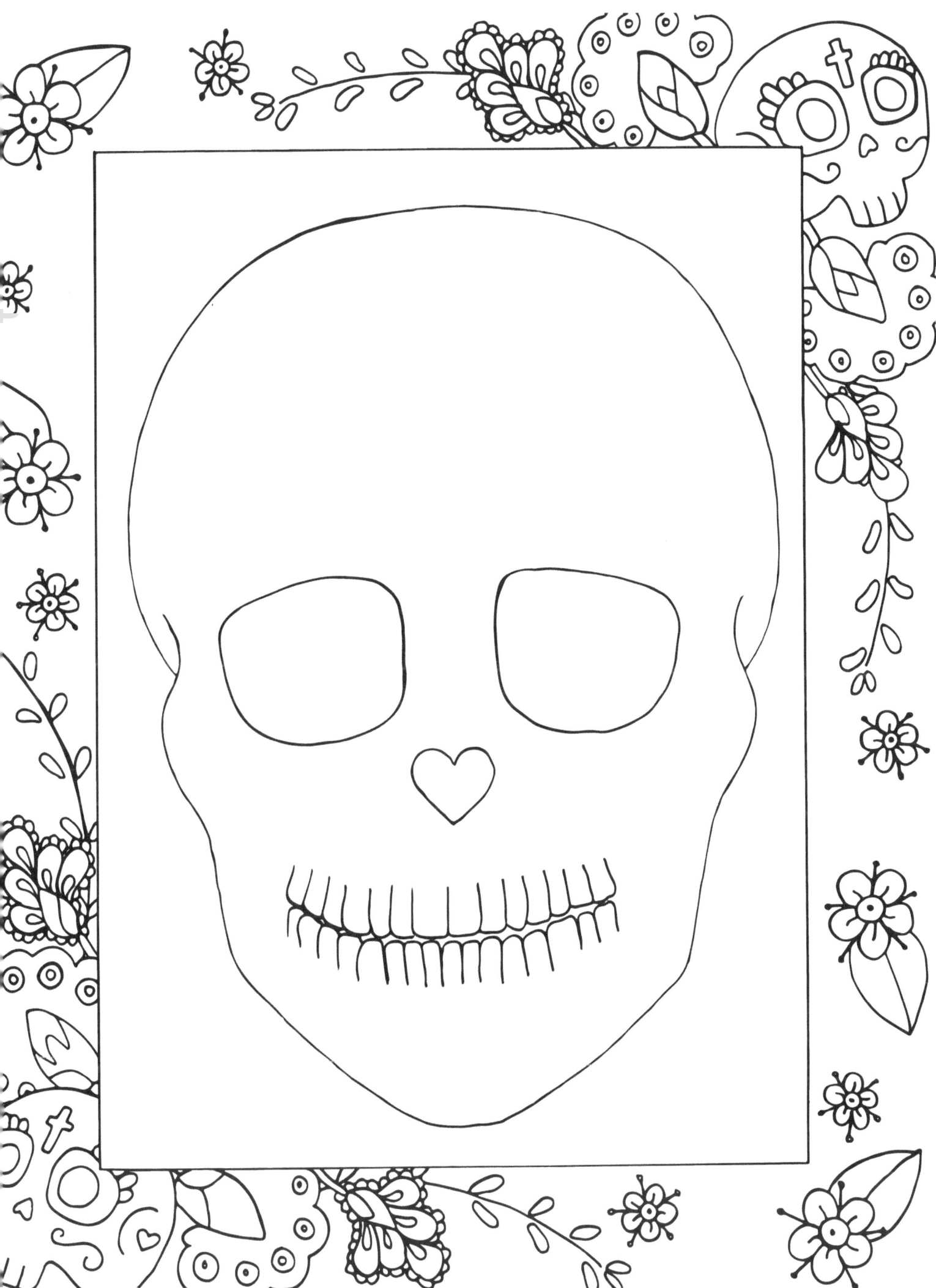

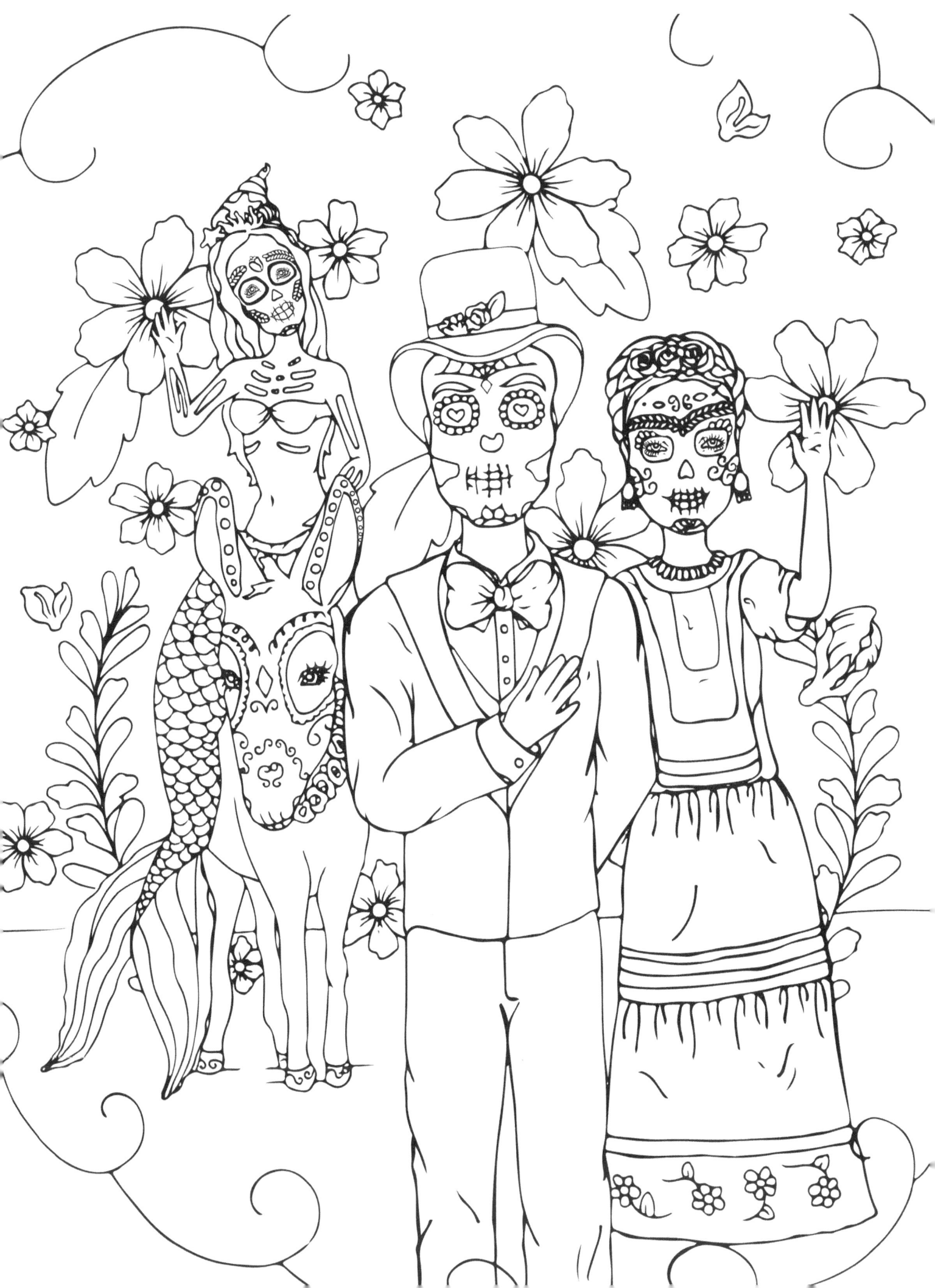

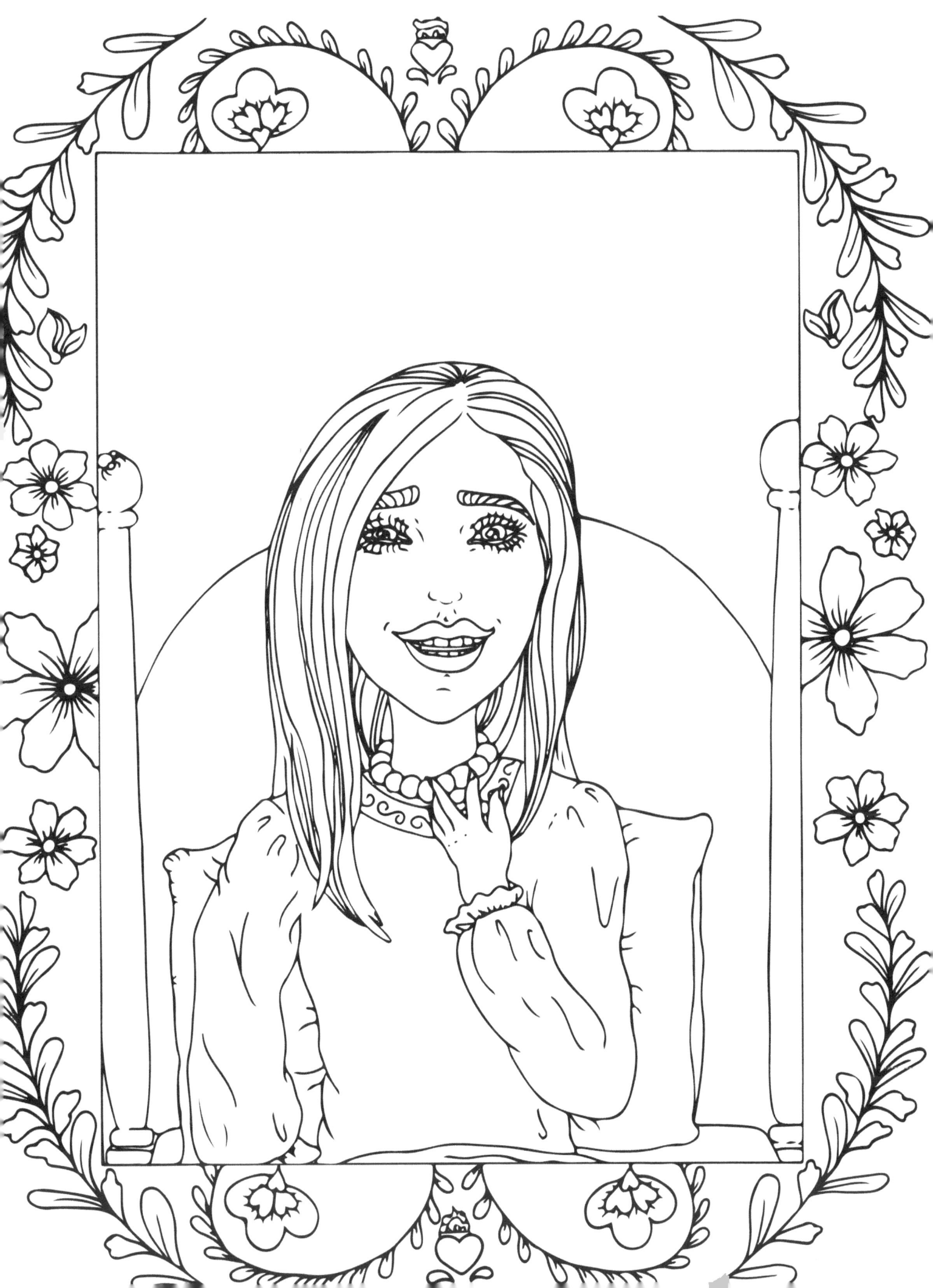

About the Artist

HI, THEre! I'm Natalie, a self-proclaimed artist, writer, blogger, and philanthropist from Southern California. I'm a mom, wife, daughter, sister, and overly enthusiastic animal lover. When I'm not hanging out with my family, writing, or drawing, I can usually be found with my nose stuck in a book or dancing around my kitchen to oldies music.

My mission to use art as a form of creative expression, self-development, and meditation can be seen first-hand on my blog at www.NatalieBorges.com.

I believe creativity is inspiration made manifest and that all of us have the potential for creativity within us. I hope you've enjoyed this coloring book and that you'll share your art and story with me on my blog or my Facebook page by heading to www.Facebook.com/natalieborges.art, where you can get the latest news on my next coloring book!